a *for* authors book

AF799912

Instagram *for* Authors

A Quick Primer for Busy *Writers*

Jenny Kate

Copyright © 2022 Jenny Kate

All rights reserved. No part of this book may be reproduced in any form or by any electronic or mechanical means, including information storage and retrieval systems, without permission in writing from the publisher, except by reviewers, who may quote brief passages in a review.

This publication is designed to provide accurate and authoritative information in regard to the subject matter covered. It is sold with the understanding that the publisher and author are not engaged in rendering legal, accounting, or other professional services. If legal or other expert assistance is required, the services of a competent professional should be sought.

Editing by Sandra Wendel, Write On, Inc.
Cover design by Ronnie Walter
Interior Design by Siva Ram Maganti

Published by
Mustard Couch Press, a subsidiary of TJC Enterprises, LLC
2308 Mt Vernon Ave #440
Alexandria, VA 22301

Web: Visit www.thewriternation.com and sign up for Writer Nation news.
Twitter: @writernationjen
Instagram: @writernationjen
Facebook.com/WriterNation
Facebook.com/groups/WriterNation
Email: writernationjen@gmail.com

Praise for "Social Media for Authors: Book Marketing for Writers Who'd Rather Write"

"A lifeline! Jenny's advice is clear, sensible, and immediately applicable." – *Barbara, author*

"I furiously scribbled notes from this book - stuff I wanted to try, things I hadn't even considered, and best or (better) practices for activities I was already doing." – *Becky Clark, author of the "Mystery Writer's Mysteries" series and the "Crossword Puzzle Mysteries."*

"An excellent wavetop introduction to developing and honing marketing skills." - *Nick Hight, author of the historical fiction thriller "Vendetta."*

"Little gem!" – *Alissa Sherry, author*

"I was always intimidated and overwhelmed with the idea of marketing my own books, but I considered every one of her small steps, and I find myself thinking: I can do this! Very useful book for a first-time author like me who was always reluctant around social media marketing." – *Marion Holt, debut author*

"What I have needed for a very long time. Now I can cope with creating a presence on social media and still have time to write." – *Carole Anne Carr, author*

"Fantastic breakdown of what to do and why. My engagement went up 10% in the first week!" – *AJ Scudiere, multi-award-winning author of 30 books*

For Writers Who'd Rather Write

Contents

"I've learned that people will forget what you said and what you did, but people will never forget how you made them feel."

—Maya Angelou

Introduction: Why Instagram

- Best Reasons to Be on Instagram
- Instagram Overview
- Best Content

I love Instagram! It's also referred to IG, so I'll use both interchangeably. Instagram, as a social media destination, is full of photos, videos, and all kinds of entertaining stuff. It's just a fun place to be. Travelers post beaches, mountains, cool architecture, famous museums. Readers post their favorite books. Runners post photos of their latest race or trail. Celebrities use live video to talk directly to their fans. Pet owners even create Instagram handles for their pets and all the antics that go with the pet. Reels are just seconds of pure fun.

Clubhouse and TikTok both made a run at hottest social media in 2021, but Instagram stayed the course, and, for now, it is a platform that can't be ignored in the United States by small business owners, a.k.a. writers. It hit the one billion follower mark in

2019 and shows no sign of stopping. As of early 2022, Instagram is the fourth most popular social media platform in the world behind only Facebook, YouTube, and WhatsApp. According to Statista, it is the second-most popular platform in the United States with nearly half the population using it, and its growth continues. It's the ninth most searched term on Google and has more daily users than TikTok, Twitter, Pinterest, and Snapchat.

That being said, TikTok is rising fast. The hashtag #booktok is exploding over at TikTok, so if you're interested in that platform, check out the bonus section for more.

First, you'll need to decide whether you want to keep a personal account or switch yours to a business account. There are several benefits to switching to a business account. I'm a big believer that authors must think of themselves as small business owners on the same par that they think of themselves as artists. If you want to make a living selling books, there is no way around it. For that reason alone, I recommend a business account. It gives you credibility as a business owner.

But for more practical business reasons, you should make the switch. You'll get data analytics that are invaluable to tracking what works and what doesn't for your posts. Understanding how your posts perform is essential to gaining followers and providing the content they want.

If you maintain a personal account, you are not able to schedule content that posts automatically. Business accounts can, using a third-party tool like Later or Hootsuite. You'll also have a contact button on your profile, which is helpful for followers to reach you. While you can create ads on Instagram with a personal account, you still need a Facebook Business Page to do it. If you have an IG business account, that's all you need.

As of the writing of this book, the most annoying thing you'll find when you switch to a business account is a loss of reach. The algorithm limits the number of business posts in the Feed. For this reason, you may consider keeping a personal account until you hit a solid number of followers. But this is also why hashtag usage is so important. Up to thirty hashtags can be used in the caption or a comment. Hashtags are how users find products they like. #Love was the most-used hashtag in 2021. How great for romance authors! #Art was in the top 10.

Best Reasons to Be on Instagram

To start, I don't think everyone needs to be on Instagram. It's a fun place, but if you've cultivated an audience elsewhere and that's still working for you, stay there. No need to start over on Instagram simply because it's a platform everyone is talking about. Let's face it, you want writing time. Adding another social outlet will bleed into that writing time for little return.

However, if you are looking for a new social outlet, then I wholeheartedly recommend Instagram. It's like Facebook, TikTok, Twitter, YouTube, and Snapchat all in one place. That might be stretching it a bit, but it's a pretty interactive environment that has something for everyone.

The average reader in the United States reads twelve books a year, according to Pew Research. Women tend to read more than men, and lucky for you, 58% of US Instagram users are female. In addition, per Instagram for Business, 83% of people on Instagram admit they use the platform to find new products.

Instagram also has several different ways to provide content to your followers. It started out as a photo-sharing platform. It still maintains that to the tune of 95 million photos and video shared per day. But it has evolved over time. There are so many different ways to share photos beyond posting to your Feed. You can also post videos of several different lengths. If you prefer writing, then captions can become mini-blogs.

Instagram Overview

Instagram has several different aspects to it that you'll need to know. Here's a quick overview. Later chapters delve into the best practices for each of them.

First, a user on Instagram is called an Instagrammer. Specialty Instagrammers have other fun designators. Those who post about books and give book reviews are bookstagrammers. Travelers post #Travelgrams. You get the idea. Instagrammers build **profiles**. Those profiles include a profile photo, a solid bio, and a link. Chapter 1 discusses all things profile to help you build the best profile for your author brand.

Next, Instagram was built primarily as a mobile platform. You'll need the app on your phone or tablet. You can do some things on the desktop site, but you still can't post photos and video from there. You can't post to your **Story** without being on a mobile device. Stories is a feature that lets you post photos or video that will stay in your Story for twenty-four hours and then disappear. This is Instagram's direct attempt to take over the Snapchat crowd. Stories are discussed in detail in chapter 2.

Stories can be posted to **Highlights**, and they will stay on the Highlights until you take them off rather than disappearing if you only post them to your Story. Highlights are the little circles under the bio. They are a place to curate any photos or video, sort of like a photo album. I go into detail on Highlights in chapter 3.

Chapter 4 discusses your **Feed**. There are two different types of feeds. The one you scroll on for hours that shows what everyone else has posted, similar to a Facebook feed or a Twitter feed. The second one is what you post on your own profile wall.

Another aspect of Instagram is **Instagram Video**. It's exactly what it sounds like–short and long form video that can be recorded or be live. These can be posted to your Feed, Story, or Reels depending on length and your objective. **Reels** are Instagram's answer to TikTok. They are fifteen - to sixty-second video clips. You can set them to music or not. Chapter 5 is all things Instagram Video.

As you are developing your Instagram marketing plan, it's

important to understand current best practices. I go into detail on Instagram Best Practices as of early 2022 in chapter 6.

Finally, as a bonus, I included a section on TikTok at the end. TikTok is fast growing and worth paying attention to. Many authors are finding success on TikTok in 2022, but I don't recommend it as a primary social media tool yet.

Your Brand

The most important thing to remember about growing an Instagram following is this: People buy from people they know, like, and trust. It's practically a mantra in the business world. In today's world, contract workers make up nearly 43% of the workforce in an economy that is becoming more and more a gig economy. Why does that matter to you? Because the nature of how consumers buy products has changed.

People buy things that fit their identity, their values, their experience. And they want those things from people who also fit their identity, values, and experience. Do you know who the head of Amazon is? How about Microsoft? Tesla? People don't buy from the company. They buy from Jeff Bezos, Bill Gates, and Elon Musk. Readers buy what Oprah tells them. Why? Because those people have cultivated a personal brand that is almost cult-like.

I'm not telling you to go out and be a celebrity, but I am telling you to build a brand. A personal brand. Everything you post should help your reader get to know you.

Your content should also reflect the needs of your reader. What experience are you providing that reader in your books? That's what you want to reflect in your personal brand and Instagram content.

Since you are targeting readers, how do you get them to know, like, and trust you on Instagram? That is where your brand comes in. Have you really developed the brand you want for your author persona? What are you truly passionate about?

What do you want to teach, inform, entertain, or inspire in your readers? How do you want to be known?

That is important because your brand is not simply colors and logos. It's what you provide to the reader. It's the passion and energy you give the world. Whether you're a nonfiction author solving a problem or a fiction author providing escapism, the brand is defined by what you offer.

So what do you offer?

Once you figure that out, then you can start creating content.

Once you do that, you can incorporate it into the content you provide. There are a million ideas for authors, but here are just a few. More content ideas can be found in chapter 6.

- Do a live weekly reading from your book.
- Post daily Reels showing what your character is doing today.
- Feed posts of places where you're researching for your book.
- Provide daily Stories of you doing something you enjoy.
- Do you use a particular pen or notebook? Talk about why on Reels.
- Do you love the color blue? Theme your Feed all in blue.
- Do you have an interesting hobby? Perfect for Stories.

The bottom line with content is that it must match and be part of your brand. If it isn't, then it doesn't meet readers' expectations. You are creating an expectation when you create a brand. Once you've done that, you need to be consistent and meet the demand. The reader needs to know what to expect when they show up on your page. So, before you jump into creating content, create the brand first. Then match the content to the brand.

"A good photograph is one that communicates a fact, touches the heart, and leaves the viewer a changed person for having seen it."

–Irving Penn

Your Instagram Profile

- Profile Pic
- A Solid Bio
- Link Trees
- Emojis

Your profile is one of the first parts of your Instagram that will attract followers. It needs to be complete and professional. It also needs to be super clear that you are an author providing a certain experience. Be very clear on that experience. For example, Author Diana Gabaldon: I write steamy, sexy Scottish romances. Or Author Diana Gabaldon–writer of steamy, sexy Scottish romance.

Your Profile Pic

Your profile photo is the first image people see. It needs to be a face. If you're writing under a pen name and would prefer not, then filter it with a pencil sketch. But studies show a face is more inviting and results in more followers than no face.

Users follow accounts with faces 80% more than those without a face. Let your photo reflect your brand. Are you a horror writer? Then a big smile is probably not sending the message you want to send. Are you a romance writer? Then a scowl doesn't really scream "happily ever after." Think about the message your facial expression sends and pick an appropriate one for your profile photo.

And a quick word about pics. This needs to be a professional photo. Not necessarily a formal headshot, but it does need to be taken by a professional with a professional camera. This should not be an iPhone image with half your friend cropped out of it. This same photo should be on all of your social platforms and other marketing material. Being an author is a profession, and whether we like it or not, professionals still need professional photos (and websites, but that's for another book).

A Solid Bio

When you think about writing your bio, think about it like a reader would. What does a reader get from you? Mystery? Horror? Knitting? Alabama football? That needs to be clear also. Your bio needs to clearly state you are an author in a specific genre. It also needs to state if you'll be talking or sharing anything else.

- Author Jane Doe
- Quirky small-town cozy mystery writer

As you're writing your bio, think like the reader. What will they see as they scroll mindlessly through their Feed? If it's your name but no descriptor, they are very likely to skip over it. But if your name includes "author," "writer," or "book" anywhere, you'll grab their attention long enough to bring them to your Feed to check if you're someone they'd like to read. The additional hobbies you include also entice readers to see if they have a connection with you, so make sure to include them. Use a couple of hashtags (not so many it's unreadable). This helps readers find you.

Remember, white space is your friend.

It's easier to read.

It's easier to scroll through.

Help readers decide quickly.

See how that is written above? Almost blog style. That's how you want the majority of your bio to look.

Finally, the last line of your bio needs a call to action, before you include your website. What do you want people to do with that website? Grab a freebie? Read an excerpt? Remember that people do not have tons of time. They are generally on and off your Feed in about three seconds, so if the call to action is not clear, you'll lose them. The link you provide needs to go to your website or your link tree (see next section). Below is an example of a full bio. The asterisks denote where an emoji could be used.

- Author Jane Doe
- Quirky small-town cozy mystery writer
- *Snowboarder
- *California girl
- Grab a free copy of my book *Breaking the Moon Lasso*
- www.mywebsite.com

Link Trees

Rather than one website, some authors like to use link trees instead. A link tree is one personalized webpage where you can share several different weblinks. For example, on IG link tree, I have a link to my latest blog post, a link to my Amazon Page, a link to my marketing quiz and a link to my latest podcast. These links are all in one place. I'm a fan on link trees, because you can offer several things at once. But there is debate. Too many choices and followers will balk. One choice limits them but only makes them click once.

I advise you to test it out and see which way works for you. But if you do use a link tree, providing no more than five links is good, so you don't overwhelm the reader. If you can't figure out how to do it on your own website, there are free tools you can use.

What you don't want to do is make the only link you provide the one to your Amazon sales page. That's like screaming "Buy my book." We'll get into the sales funnel in chapter 6, but the top of the funnel is where you woo your follower to become a reader. To do that, you want to provide something of worth before going in for the sale. You want to build a rapport with the reader. Think of a first date. You don't ask your date to marry you. You drink wine and take a walk and get to know them.

This is also true with bringing in new readers. Offering a first in the series free or a novella or something fun like sketches, maps, or quizzes helps bring in your reader by providing them an opportunity to get to know your work before they go all in and start buying everything.

There are a gazillion books in the world. Your job as the author (after writing the book) is to get it into the hands of readers. You can't do that without offering them something different. There are too many free books available, and you're competing against too many odds not to offer something else.

Like, know, and trust. That's the name of the game. Get a reader to like, know, and trust you, and you'll sell books. Do that by offering interesting and fun content. The link you include in your Instagram bio should be an opening into the world you are building for the reader.

A Word on Emojis

Emojis are those little cartoons you can add to the bio. Use them. Why? Because this isn't your stuffy great-grandparents' era of propriety and stodginess. We live in the 2020s where things go fast and emojis help explain things faster than words. I know, that one is tough for readers, but it's the truth.

Instagram is supposed to be fun. Emojis help make it fun. I like to use them like bullet points.

 A stack of books in front of "Reader."

 A pen in front of "Writer."

 A football or an elephant in front of "Bama fan." 

"Storytelling is the most powerful way to put ideas into the world today."

—Robert McKee

Instagram Stories

- What Is a Story?
- Why Should I Post?
- When Should I Post?
- What Should I Post?

Ever heard of Snapchat but don't really know what it is? It's video clips that disappear after a certain amount of time. Stories are Instagram's attempt to snag a younger market–the Snapchat market–and continue its growth. That may be its original intent, but Instagrammers have come to embrace Stories. They are simply easy ways for people to get to know you without having to worry about production quality.

What Is a Story?

If you look at the profile pics of fellow Instagrammers, some have a little circle around their photo and others don't. The ones with circles have uploaded a Story, visible to anyone. Stories are basically little glimpses into people's lives. This is where you don't have to have the curated look of a profile page or a polished video production. You can be real and fun.

Stories are short fifteen-second clips. They disappear after twenty-four hours on the profile. You can add to them all day long. It's a great way to continue to provide content with relatively little effort.

Why Should I Post?

You should post to Stories because Instagram saw a thirty-minute uptick in usage of the platform after they implemented Stories, according to HubSpot. Clearly, users like them. They are a very good answer to the short attention spans of modern humans. If you want someone to sit down and actually read a book, you're going to have to get their attention first. This is how to do it.

When Should I Post?

Stories disappear in twenty-four hours, so time your posts for the optimal slots to upload them. I used to tell people to chase the times when people are on the platform. For the record, that tends to be middle of the week, middle of the day for Instagram. That being said, by using hashtags, locations, and tags for other users, I'm not sold on the idea that it matters when you upload a new Story. I think you'd rather be writing, so upload at the time of day you have time to upload.

If you are launching a book and coming up to publication date, you'll want to post every day during the week. But if you're in writing, or in editing mode, then once every few days works. The deal with Instagram is to consistently post across all avenues. That means if you lay off Stories for a few days but post to your Feed or do a Reel, then you should still see consistent engagement and views for your IG. Stories are actually great for the quick hit when you don't have time to write a full caption for a Feed photo or don't feel like messing with Reels or IGTV, so I encourage more usage of Stories when you don't have a lot of time.

What Should I Post?

This goes back to your brand and your attempt to help readers like, know, and trust you. What are you offering your reader? What experience are you trying to build? What do you want them to know about you, your characters, and your books? That's what you post.

Sometimes this simply might be ten seconds of why your character hates eggs for breakfast. I take a daily walk and post fun, amusing, or interesting things I see on my walk. Today's walk generated a quick video of a UPS truck with reggae music blaring from it. Yesterday it was video of a cute little dog chasing a ball with his owner. Stories are the place to post whatever you feel like because it allows the reader to get to know you. It doesn't have to be overly thought out or planned. Save that for live videos, Reels, and your Feed.

"Marketing is really just about sharing your passion."

– Michael Hyatt,
NY Times Best Selling Author

Instagram Highlights

- What Is a Highlight?
- Why Should I Have Highlights?
- How Do I Make Highlights?
- What Should Be in Highlights?

A lot of Instagrammers miss the Highlights. They just simply don't use the option. I don't know why, but it's a super easy way to gain credibility on the platform. If you have Highlights on your profile page, you look like you know how to use IG. It's also a pretty easy way to gain engagement. You can promote a book launch or offer a quiz or a sneak peek into an event you're holding. But let's not get ahead of ourselves.

What Is a Highlight?

Remember how your Stories disappear after twenty-four hours? Highlights are Stories that stay until you remove them. You find them below your profile pic. They are the little circles in a long row under your bio. If you create a Story for your characters in a particular book, then all of those in one place makes for a great Highlight.

Why Should I Have Highlights?

Good question. Because they provide a place for you to archive your best Stories. Think of Highlights as the highlight reel of your daily Stories or a photo album of all your best work. You can create category Highlights.

I have Highlights of my favorite travel places. I have one Highlight with several Stories that ask readers questions so it's fun and interactive. Still another is about bookstores, and I post to it every time I go to the bookstore or find a new one. Because you can change the covers and the Highlight names, it's a really cool place to upload similar Stories.

Even more important, this content is good for new readers to help get to know, like, and trust you. Highlights show your activities and interests. They showcase your books and, just frankly, provide more opportunity for a reader to get to know you.

How Do I Make Highlights?

Once you have a Story, you can choose to make it a Highlight. At the bottom of your Story screen, just click Highlight and either add it to an existing Highlight or create a new one. One of the features that tripped me up was creating Highlight cover images. I like a clean look where each cover is similar. If you just upload your Stories, then they'll all be different. Creating a similar icon image as your Highlight covers is another chance to showcase your brand colors and provide a smooth title page for your Highlight.

You can easily create these in Canva—an online graphics tool. Believe me, if I can use Canva, anyone can. You simply create the graphic, save it to your phone, and go into IG to edit the Highlight, edit the cover, and upload the photo. It's that easy.

What Should Be in Highlights?

A curated collection of your Stories. Once you figure out which categories you want to create in your Highlights, then you can figure out which Stories go in there. You can also start creating Stories to match the Highlights so you can add them later.

Writers can create Highlights for all sorts of topics: research destinations and interesting information, quizzes to see which character your reader most relates to, your books, your freebies. Make this part of your marketing plan.

"Your brand is what people say about you when you're not in the room."

–Jeff Bezos, Founder & CEO, Amazon

Instagram Feed

- What Is the Feed?
- What Should I Post?
- Different Themes to Use
- When Should I Post?

The Feed is not the most important part of your Instagram. That's why I didn't put it in chapter 1. How many times do you go to your favorite author's Instagram Feed? Probably once or never. That's because you're scrolling through. You can see the content in your own scrolling, whether it's a photo or Reel or live video, and if you're flipping through Stories, you'll see it there. That doesn't mean the Feed isn't important, it's just not the most important thing.

What Is the Feed?

The Feed is your home page on Instagram. It's where readers go to see your bio, your bio pic, your Highlights, Reels, and the content you've put in your Feed (photos, videos). Back in the day, a fully curated, themed-out IG page was all the rage.

It's basically building an overall aesthetic using consistent themes. Those themes could include using the same color in your posts or the same style, angle or landscape. That's a ton of work. And today, not completely necessary. You can still create a consistent aesthetic without being relentless about it.

That does not mean you shouldn't think about the Feed. But it does mean you don't need to stress about having the most curated, professional-quality Feed. Focus on having an aesthetically pleasing board and the caption that goes with each post.

The board is the top nine posts people see when they first click to your page. This page is the first glimpse people get at what you post. If it's a mess of photos in all colors and scattered about, then it probably won't be visually pleasing. Go back to your brand. What colors did you decide reflect your brand? What logos? This is where you can show this off.

Decide your aesthetic and create something that pulls a reader in. Make it visually pleasing so they'll click follow.

My photographer friend calls it window shopping. If someone clicks on your home page or Feed and can't figure out what's going on because there is just too much, they might click away. But if it's visually pleasing, they'll start looking through your posts and probably follow you. You'll have two or three seconds to grab a follower's attention and help them decide to click. That's why the Feed is important.

What Should I Post?

Photos, videos, logos, books, pets, travel. Figure out what your brand stands for and focus on that. You don't need more than three to five "items" you routinely post. Package them according to your brand colors and you're all set. Do you have a plan? Get one. Your Feed is where you can spend some time really thinking about what you want to post and what you want your reader to get out of it.

Photos and videos should reflect your brand. I know you've

heard it a million times, but there's no escaping this. You must post what reflects your brand. Similar colors. Similar styles. Similar themes.

More importantly than the aesthetic is the caption. The caption to your photos is almost a mini-blog where you get to talk to your readers. This is where you really get to shine. You're a writer. Time to write!

But this isn't fiction writing. It's copywriting. It's marketing. Use emojis, subheads, bullet points. White space is your friend, but these can still be rather long. You can make a point with these, so write one in a format readers can get through quickly.

This section is where we need to talk about brand photography. Brand photography is when a professional photographer takes photos of you specifically for social media. Entrepreneur Amy Porterfield has quarterly photo sessions so she always has fresh photos to use.

Do you need this? No, you can create photos and a Feed without it. You can do a batch session where a friend takes some photos of you to use over the next month or so. Photos with a face receive 38% more engagement on Instagram, so I do recommend photos of you. By batching them, you will have them on hand when you're ready to post or when you schedule posts using a third-party scheduler like Later or Hootsuite or Sprout Social.

But if you do decide to hire a professional photographer, make sure they do brand photography. This isn't a wedding. It's not the fall family photos where everyone is throwing leaves. This is professional photography of you to market and sell you and your books.

There is some argument about the type of photos released by the photographer. Do you need license to post? Yes. Do they all need to be professionally edited? No. This is social media, not a glossy brochure or a wedding album. Should you be able to make outfit changes? Yes. This is where things get a bit sticky because the need hasn't quite caught up with the industry, and some photographers balk at multiple wardrobe changes.

For a quarterly photo shoot, you need at least thirty images in different poses, locations, and outfits. It shouldn't take more than an hour or an hour and a half. I've been charged anywhere from $200 to $1,600. The best bang for my buck was an hour in Franklin, Tennessee, where I wore layers and changed in and out of those layers and got forty photos and paid $500.

Make sure you find someone who understands what small business, brand photography is. But don't waste their time either. Wild wardrobe changes that take a lot of time waste the photographer's time, and it wastes yours. Pick a location with several different options: coffee shops, libraries, nooks and crannies off the street.

Regardless of whether you have photos taken by a professional or by a friend, it is a good idea to have a batch ready to work with so you aren't scrambling for content.

Different Themes to Use

I included this section because reception to IG Feeds continually evolves. A couple of years ago, themes on Instagram Feeds were all about the grid. Every other photo was a similar aesthetic. Then it was all about the color. All photos had one particular color pop in the post. Now it's all about the mood board. What mood do you want to reflect?

Go back to your brand and that will help you. I'm also a big fan of researching authors similar to you and see what they're doing. You might also research big names in the industry to see how they are posting.

The aesthetic, while not as important as it used to be, can still be fun to play around with. Ideas include all black-and-white photos, or only photos where you are wearing red. Maybe you like the outdoors, so all your photos are outdoors. Do you have a pet? Readers love pets, so photos of your pet and you with your pet are always killing it on Instagram. You can also photograph your book in all your favorite places. The ideas are endless. Just make sure to plan it out.

When Should I Post?

Two or three times a week. Yep, that's it. The algorithm values video over Feed posts. That's why you can really think through the content on the Feed post and be really intentional on what you offer. You'll spend more of your time posting other content than photos in the Feed. These can also be scheduled with a scheduler like Hootsuite, Later, or Sprout Social.

If you have a business account, the scheduler will post for you. If you're still on a personal account, you'll get a message when it's time to post, and you'll need to go in and post yourself.

"I do video because I love connecting with my audience. I love being able to deliver a message in a way that really makes an impact."

–Amy Porterfield, founder Online Marketing Made Easy & marketing expert

Instagram Video

- Why Should I Use Instagram Video?
- What is Instagram Video?
- How to Use Videos, Reels, and Live

Why Should I Use Instagram Video?

Video is king on the internet. There is no way around it. Omnicore Agency reports YouTube is the second-most visited website and the second-most used social platform in the world. Video production company Lemonlight reports that 84% of consumers (think readers) admit that watching brand videos convinced them to buy a product. A Renderforest survey found that 78% of video content makers received more traffic to their websites with video than before they used video. They also found that, by far, video is the number-one type of content people prefer with 81% of users reporting a preference for video.

All of these statistics and more convinced Instagram to prioritize videos. That has paid off. Instagram reports an increase in traffic since the push to focus on video. It also reports videos receive more than twice the engagement than photos.

If you're thinking you simply don't want to make or learn how to make videos, I'll say this: if you have a phone, you can make a video. Do you have to be in them? No. Although faces receive 38% more engagement than photos and videos without faces, you definitely do not have to be the star of all your videos. Your voice would be helpful though.

Remember, the objective here is to find a way for readers to like, know, and trust you. Then turn those readers into fans, and eventually into superfans. If you don't feel like being in front of the camera is for you, then narrating the video is the next best thing.

If you consider podcasting statistics, they are a good comparison to encourage you to think about at least narrating your own videos. Podcasting listeners increased from 25 million to 116 million from 2013 to 2021, and that number is expected to be 136 million by 2024, according to Business Insider Intelligence.

Let's get into what video is available on Instagram and how to use it.

What Is Instagram Video?

Instagram now offers three ways to upload video to the platform: Stories, Reels, and Instagram Video. Stories are Instagram's answer to Snapchat. Reels are similar to TikToks. Loosely, Instagram Video can be compared to YouTube and YouTube Live. See how IG wants to take over the entire video ecosystem? This is one of the reasons I like and use Instagram. The platform provides access to just about any content type available on the internet all in one place. And the reach is totally worth it. So, let's dive a little deeper.

Stories were discussed in chapter 2. But as a refresher, Stories are those fifteen-second video clips that disappear after twenty-four hours. If you want them to last longer, you can add them to your Highlights (chapter 3). To find out if anyone has a Story posted, look to see if there is a pink or red circle around the bio photo. If so, then that user has posted to their Story.

There are several ways to promote your Stories so more people use them. Include hashtags, but not a lot of them. One or two works fine. Unless they are part of your headline, make them small or hide them under a sticker. Stickers are enhancements you can include in your story to make it more fun. It isn't necessary for your follower to see the hashtag. You are using it, in this case, to alert the IG algorithm you have something to share under that hashtag.

Another way to promote your Stories for more engagement is to link your Instagram account to Facebook account. Then your users will see the Stories on both Facebook or Instagram.

Stories are the ideal way for your readers to get to know you. If your IG Feed is curated with a consistent theme, and always has a purpose for your business, it's harder for readers to really get to know you because the content you share is buttoned up. However, these little clips on your Stories provide insights into how you spend your day, what hobbies you are into, and can really show what you're into. It's a great way to share without sharing everything.

Reels are Instagram's answer to TikTok. They are shorter, up to sixty-second, vertical video clips that appear in the Feed if you want them to and in the Reels tab. (The Reels tab looks like a movie set clapper icon.) Reels are simply fun. This is the time to show your personality. Does this mean you need to sing and dance? No. I've seen history professors give quick lessons on history. Docents give museum tours. And fiction writers read their books, interview their characters, and discuss their world building. Nonfiction authors teach something, discuss research or facts, or read from their book.

Reels differ from Stories in several ways. First, they don't disappear in twenty-four hours. Second, the Reels platform offers quite a few more creative tools to help you create cleaner videos with more effects. Third, Reels can be posted to Stories or your Feed or, in some cases, be featured in the Explore section of Instagram. The Explore section is a search function like Google, and includes top hashtags or trends to help Instagrammers find something. Reels also have their own dedicated section on Instagram, so you or your followers can scroll through IG Reels for hours if you want.

Instagram Videos are longer-form video, up to ten minutes (some verified accounts can go up to an hour). Instagram Live is exactly what it sounds like. You can stream live up to four hours on the platform. Both will appear on your Feed wall, although the live stream will only stay available for followers to watch for thirty days.

How to Use Videos, Reels, and Live

Before you create any video content, it is essential to plan. I know we'll have some pantser turn squeamish at that, but this isn't writing. This is marketing. What are you trying to accomplish with your Story, Reel, or Video? Are you posting so readers will like, know, and trust you? There is a lot of flexibility if this is the answer. Hobbies, behind-the-scenes, daily encounters, and things you find funny, compelling, scary, interesting are just some examples of potential events you can video and post in any of the four venues.

What if you're advertising a book launch or freebie? Then you might do a weekly live show where you read a portion of your book. Or you might post a Reel of your book launch party location. If it's virtual, then the room you'll be in is fun.

Whatever you post, you don't need fancy equipment. You need a plan. Create a content plan quarterly so you aren't scrambling for what to post. Allow flexibility because Reels, just like Stories, can feel a lot more spontaneous than live or videos, so play around with that. Have fun with it. This is a social networking platform. It's supposed to be fun. For more on what to post and best practices, read the next chapter.

"We sell feelings, status, and connection,
not tasks or stuff."

–Seth Godin, marketing super expert

Best Practices

- Grow Your Following
- Content Ideas
- Captions
- Advertising

When you think about best practices on Instagram, think about why you want to grow your following. You want to find readers. You want to sell books. Right? Instagram offers what modern consumers want. Attention. The insights into your writing life and the "exclusives" they get about your books and characters give readers the inside scoop they crave. If you use any of the video platforms, more's the better.

Grow Your Following

Growing followers on Instagram is a lot like growing followers on any platform. You need to follow others and engage with your followers' posts. But be deliberate about your own engagement. Don't just double tap on a photo and call it good.

Make sure the account you're following fits your brand. Read the caption or watch their videos and make a substantive contribution in the comments. I know I've said this before, but it's like dating. Get to know them and let them get to know you.

As you think about growing your following, think about the sales funnel. The top of the funnel is where you grab their attention. If you ask readers straight out to buy your book (the bottom of the sales funnel), the likely answer is no. Readers want to buy from people they like, know, and trust. So give them that first—content that helps them get to know you. If we take the example of a date and apply it to the sales funnel, it will help to understand.

The top of the sales funnel is where the couple meets. They circle around each other, flirt a little bit, and maybe have coffee. Discussions at this stage are usually limited to favorite colors and movies and maybe hobbies. If the conversation proves fruitful, there may be a second date. To make the conversation fruitful for a reader, authors need to provide fun, entertaining, or inspiring tidbits about their brand. What are you passionate about? Don't give away all the details, just a few things to keep the other person interested.

If the second date happens or the reader decides to click follow, now we're moving down the funnel. The date has become a night at the movies or a ballgame. We're not meeting the parents yet. Still getting to know each other. For an author, that can be continuing to provide interesting content about your books and hobbies. If the reader downloads your novella or character sketch, now you're building a fan. On the next date, we're headed to maybe a weekend trip together. For a reader, it's time to turn that fan into a superfan.

Invite your fans to your exclusive street team, reader group, or advanced reader copy squad. Show them all the freebies and insider information they'll receive. Make them part of your world.

By this time, you're almost to the bottom of the funnel. All this time you are continuing to post content that is educational, fun, interesting, and free. Readers are getting to know you through your Stories and Reels and Instagram Live videos. It's like your date bringing flowers or sending short texts every day—still doing the work but not meeting the parents.

But now it's time. The followers who engage with your content, download your freebie, join your reader group are ripe for the asking. Let them meet the parents. Send them the book launch information for preorders and ask for a review of the free novella or book they downloaded during the second date. Then start over. Back at the top of the funnel with more "dating" content to keep them interested.

Make sure you post often and in varying types of content. Use all available platforms on IG—your Feed, Stories, Reels, Highlights, video, photos, and captions. Does this mean you need to post every hour? No. But you do need to post at least once a day during the week. If you have a business account, you can schedule those posts using Later or Buffer or some other scheduler. If you have a personal account, you can still schedule posts, but they won't actually post for you. Those third-party apps will remind you to hit "post" on the content you've scheduled.

A lot of folks get right to the bottom of the funnel and ask for the buy or the review, but that's an immediate turnoff. Create the foundation that readers crave and then go for it. But you must continue to post. Be consistent and dedicated. I know it sounds like a lot to do, but there is a lot of competition. First, there are 250,000 authors registered with Draft2Digital, and they produce a lot of books. That's a lot of authors and a lot of books to compete with. Second, Instagrammers post more than 100 million photos a day and 400 million Stories. That's a lot of content to stand out it. You need to connect with readers, and the sales funnel approach is time proven by business consultants.

Content Ideas

At a loss for what to post? That's what we'll get into here. Just like video is king on the internet. So is content. You can't just slap something up there and expect people to "ooh" and "ahh" over it. They won't. Which brings me to your brand. How clear, super clear, are you on your brand? The clearer you are on your brand, the easier it will be to plan out your content.

A brand, in its simplest sense, is what you offer the reader. Start with your books. What genre do you write in? Mine that for everything you can. Romance author? Then everything to do with dating, marriage, sex, and relationships is open to you. Thriller writer? All things James Bond, spy craft, and geopolitics provide excellent resources. Do you follow the CIA on Twitter? You should. It's an amazing place to grab ideas for content.

Aside from genre, what are your hobbies or those of your characters? What do they like to eat? How do they decompress? What is a typical Friday night like for you or them? Use that for content. Where do you live? Where do your characters live? Become a local tourist and post about it. All of this is part of your brand.

Next, mine your books and your writing process. Take the time to brainstorm your brand and your books. Make a list, and from that list create a content calendar. The more you brainstorm up front, the more you plan out your content, the less a struggle it is in the end. To get you started, considering adding the following to your content plan: character sketches or interviews, maps, family trees, research material, progress reports on your current work in progress, reviews of your latest book, interviews with research subjects or other authors, discuss deleted scenes and backstory, expert quotes, results from professional studies and analysis, vintage photos (with licensed permission), and even venn diagrams. Your cover should only be used when you're ready to launch. Otherwise, it comes across as spammy.

Ask your readers or followers questions to get to know them.

Get them involved. What are their favorite books, authors, movies, scenes, characters? Best rule of thumb is 80% content for the follower. Twenty percent of the content is for you. That 20% is when you provide updates about your books, where they can buy them and when. Do this too soon and it's like asking your date to pay for the bill as soon as drinks arrive. Hard pass.

Because you are always adding new followers to your Instagram, moving them through the funnel is not linear. This is why you need so much variety in the content and the type of content.

Content ideas are developed from your brand and can be used in photos, graphics, videos, or live video.

Top of the funnel

- Your hobbies or those of your characters
- Your hometown or those of your books
- Your pets and their shenanigans
- All about writing–where you write, your favorite part, how/why you got into writing
- Your favorite anything
- Your genre and all the aspects of it
- Read your work
- Your characters–interview them, sketch them, family trees

Middle of the funnel

- Photo your book everywhere
- Quotes from your book
- Street team/reader group/ARC information
- Book review quotes

Bottom of the funnel

- Book launch info
- Buy links

Captions

Captions are a fantastic place for writers. These features are ideal for use as a mini-blog. Believe it or not, captions actually get read on Instagram. Well, good captions. Writing effective captions involves the use of copywriting techniques. Not prose. Not fiction. Copywriting.

Compelling copywriting uses the business side of your brain, not so much the creative side. You are writing for a purpose–to grab attention and keep it. You're competing with video and photos, so you need to get to the point using as few words as possible.

The first sentence in your caption is like a headline. It's what will keep them reading. I like to use a question: How's your social media game? What's your favorite book? When is the best time to write?

Even if they read nothing else, some users will feel compelled to answer that question in the comments. Use phrases and short sentences. Yes, it's perfectly fine to use phrases separated by periods. Full sentences take too much time to read. You want them to fly through this.

Use headers. These can be in all caps to help distinguish that it's a header. You can also use emojis on either side of it for the same purpose. Use bulleted lists. Emojis are great icons in place of bullets. Instagram users love emojis. Use those to your advantage.

Finally, use hashtags. While adding them throughout the caption is fine, it gets a bit cluttered and hard to read. A good best practice for hashtags is to add them at the end. Three to five is plenty. You can also "hide" the hashtags by hitting a hard return several times and adding up to thirty at the end of your caption. Yes, thirty. Don't freak out.

Using hashtags is how your post gets seen. It's how the algorithm knows to pick up your content and add it to a certain category. There is some debate on this now, but if the hashtags are hidden, the more the better. But don't make up hashtags.

Use those that are already in use. Look on other author's captions to see which ones they are using. Go to the IG Explore page and start typing a search term, you'll see hashtags there as well. I have a list on my website if you want to download it for free. If you want to create your own hashtag, that's fine, but include more well-known ones at the same time. Users won't be able to find the one you made up until it's been out a while piggy-backing on those other more used hashtags.

Advertising

To grow your following, build an email list or even use the list to sell your book, I recommend you learn how to use Instagram Ads. I go into a lot of depth on ads in my book Ads for Authors: Advertising Basics for Writers Who'd Rather Write, but here is a quick primer.

Facebook, or Meta, owns Instagram and the ads platform. The best thing about Meta's ad platform is the audience you can target. This is why you absolutely must have a clear understanding of who your ideal reader is. Having a list of comparable authors is also extremely helpful. Ads on Instagram can be placed just about anywhere–in videos, on images, in Stories. They can be carousel ads, collection ads, shopping ads. There are a lot of options.

The most important point to know about ads is you must test everything. So plan your budget accordingly. You need to test the audience and the images or video you use. You need to test the ad copy and the location. I recommend running three or four ads at once and change only one thing on each ad to see which ad resonates more. Do that three or four times to gather the data you need to then run the best ad you can.

For example, if I'm testing an image, I'll run three ads with three different images while the audience, location, and copy all remain the same. Once I have the image with the most hits, I'll move on to copy and do the same testing. Then again with audience. Once I have the data for those three items, then I run an ad with the image, copy, and audience that garnered the best results. Only then will you really start seeing results.

When those results start waning, you'll start all over. You don't need to spend a lot of money testing those ads, but know that the most effective way to get your content in front of the people who want to see it is to test ads.

Another advertising option is to simply boost content from time to time to gain engagement and further your reach. This can be done rather cheaply and you can test out which content resonates with your followers and post more of it.

That's your overview of Instagram for authors who'd rather write. Once you know your way around the platform, creating and posting will be easy for you. But wait, I have bonus material for you in the next and final chapter.

"You stand out more by being weird than fitting in."

—Emma Tupa, Product Marketing Specialist at CoSchedule

Bonus: A Quick Rundown of TikTok

- The Algorithm
- Best Practices

TikTok absolutely exploded in 2021 and will continue that trajectory into 2022. As of the writing of this book, TikTok had almost 100 million users in the United States, and 86% of those are between the ages of sixteen and forty-four. Nielsen did a study in 2021 and asked more than 8,000 TikTok users what they liked about the app. The top answers included features users appreciated about the authenticity of the app over curated, ultra-unfiltered experiences on other social sites, and the app simply makes them happy. In a world where the headlines are always awful, TikTok a nice place to escape to.

Even more useful answers to the Nielsen study were that nearly 60% agreed TikTok is a place with a sense of community, and 84% agreed there is always content they can relate to, and finally almost 80% actually read the comments on posts and videos. All of this is reason enough for you to consider TikTok as your social media platform of choice, or at least dabble with it.

It's the Wild West right now, and about the only place on the internet where organic growth still means something. Organically you can grow a following simply by posting every day or a couple of times a day or a couple of times a week. Ultra-marketer Neil Patel gives TikTok until 2023 before TikTok becomes more like other platforms and we'll start having to pay for growth, so if you're interested, now is the time to jump in.

A couple of other features to consider about TikTok. This platform is designed for the Every Person. Content is created by everyday folks, which makes it easier to go viral on TikTok. It's all about relatability, and TikTok offers it in spades. And the app isn't complicated. It is rather easy to use. If you can use any social media outlet out there, then you can use TikTok.

The Algorithm

What's special about TikTok over traditional social media is the algorithm. The way the algorithm works, your post will still be seen months later because maybe the hashtag you used or the music you added is making a comeback in engagement. Then TikTok will show it again and again. This is different from Instagram that just shows the latest posts, or Twitter that drowns you in every single tweet posted that second.

For example, TikTok will show you content that reflects what you engage with similar to other social platforms. But the algorithm also registers just how long you watched that dog post. If you didn't watch it for very long, but you did stop on the cat post longer, it will lessen the number of dog posts it shows you and increase the number of cat posts you see. If you watch all the TikToks with the song from that Irish band everyone is using, you'll start to see more and more of those posts. But if you fly through the latest Justin Bieber lip sync trend, TikTok is likely to show you less of those.

In addition, this is why you don't need a huge following to go viral. TikTok doesn't factor that in when it decides what to show. The videos are counted on their merit or content, not on your follower count.

Best Practices

Yes, TikTok is for fun and distraction, but that doesn't mean you have to sing and dance and act a fool, although some of that is fun too. TikTok content is all about small, short video clips. Think quick hits. Best length is between nine and fifteen seconds. While that sounds like no time at all, if you don't grab the user's attention in the first two seconds, they are more than likely going to keep scrolling.

The type of content that resonates on TikTok is the same that resonates anywhere. People want to be entertained. They want to learn something. But more than anything, they want a distraction from life. Your books and your brand can provide that to them. Just as I discussed Instagram content in the last chapter, that same content can be used on TikTok. Be authentic.

One of the best ways to showcase your brand or content is to stay with the trends. Set your content to the latest trending music offered by TikTok or the latest filter. Spend some time on the app looking at what is trending and brainstorm a way to use that with your brand.

On the Social Media Examiner podcast in early 2022, TikTokker Jackson Zaccaria reported three types of content have been the source of his TikTok success: short, long, and trending. Short content would be less than fifteen seconds. Long content, one to three minutes. Trending is exactly what it says, using a trend to tie back to your brand. Posting several different types of content will provide you analytics to determine what content resonates.

A hashtag you'll want to follow is #BookTok. Readers and authors have flocked to BookTok. So have TikTokkers who provide reviews on books or offer their favorite books on TikTok.

Similar to book bloggers or bookstagrammers, BookTokkers who use #BookTok to spread the word about a new book are worth paying attention to. They aren't always providing reviews.

Booktokkers do a lot more than that. Some act out their favorite literary characters. Others create memes from books or characters. Still others project fan fiction in various ways. It's fun for everyone. Study what is happening on BookTok and you'll know what content to contribute. Take advantage of the trends to increase your own following and engagement.

To create compelling TikToks, here's some functional advice. Make sure your video is vertical. Use filters, frames, and add music. Make sure the first two seconds get to the point. Write your caption with the same idea in mind. TikTok doesn't show the entire caption on the screen, so use the first three to five words to make your point. Be concise. Use a header. This is a great way to get your point across quickly so users will know right off the bat what you're providing. Provide a call to action: tell the user exactly what you want them to do with the video, if anything. The 80-20 rule still applies. Eighty percent of your TikToks should provide engaging, interesting content so users get to know, like, and trust you. The other 20% can include calls to action to buy your book, follow you, sign up for an email, whatever. Be sparing about these.

Last tip: post regularly. As with any social media strategy, post consistently. Jackson Zaccaria admitted to posting several times a day. But sisters Caroline Peckham and Susanne Valenti, TikTok superstars and fiction authors, admit to posting only a few times a week. They had seven books listed as number-one bestsellers in various Amazon genres and attribute TikTok to some of that success.

Final Thoughts

TikTok will continue to grow over time. As of January 2022, it has over a billion users. It was the most downloaded app worldwide in 2020 and 2021. Bloomberg reports TikTok users spend over an hour on the platform every day.

I recommend spending time with the app. Learn its functionality, and discover all the trends. Find users who put out content similar to what you want to put out. Also look for users similar in personality to you and pay attention to how they are presenting content. This will make it easier to get started.

Before I sign off, a quick word about controversy. TikTok is owned by ByteDance, a Chinese company and its ownership has garnered some debate. India permanently banned the app in January 2021 after a border dispute with China. There is some consternation in the US about TikTok for security reasons. I specifically asked a computer security professional friend of mine if he had any concerns about downloading TikTok to his device and he said no. For those concerned about security, he recommended using an old smartphone. But he had no other concerns.

TikTok is definitely the social platform to watch in 2022. Even if you decide not to engage, pay attention to where it's going. You might decide later to engage. If you stick with Instagram and post a lot of Reels, that is good practice for posting to TikTok. So if, or when, you're ready to make the jump, you'll be ready to go.

About the Author

Jenny Kate has been a communicator, marketer, teacher, and public relations professional since 2001. She has party planned for the US Ambassador to Portugal, managed location production for Hollywood filmmakers, and eaten Taco Bell with a famous late-night television host. She has provided speech input to the President of the United States, has been quoted by the *New York Times*, CNN, Fox News, and *Time* and provided research opportunities for writers, professors, documentary filmmakers, and members of Congress.

With her husband, she cofounded *Writer Nation*, an online community for writers providing essential marketing tips and advice for building an author platform and for finding more readers.

An Alabama-born girl, she bleeds crimson and white. When she isn't writing or teaching about marketing, she travels the world looking for the world's best vegan sandwich. So far, tofu banh mi in Hoi An, Vietnam, is winning that race.

She is the author of *Social Media for Authors: Marketing for Writers Who'd Rather Write* and *Ads for Authors: Advertising*

Basics for Writers Who's Rather Write and the forthcoming book *Author Brands: Build an Identity for Your Business.*

Sign up for her monthly newsletter at www.thewriternation.com

Feel free to reach out anytime with marketing or publishing questions:

Web: www.thewriternation.com
Twitter: @writernationjen
Instagram: @writernationjen
Facebook.com/WriterNation
Facebook.com/groups/WriterNation
Email: writernationjen@gmail.com

Made in the USA
Monee, IL
04 November 2026

67382314R00036